通向中国

Chinese Odyssey
Innovative Chinese Courseware

SIMPLIFIED & TRADITIONAL

Vol. 1 • WORKBOOK

Xueying Wang, Li-chuang Chi, and Liping Feng

王学英　　祁立庄　　冯力平

 CHENG & TSUI COMPANY Boston

The contents of *Chinese Odyssey* were developed in part under a grant from the Fund for the
Improvement of Postsecondary Education (FIPSE), U.S. Department of Education. However,
these contents do not necessarily represent the policy of the Department of Education, and
you should not assume endorsement by the Federal Government.

12 11 10 09 08   2 3 4 5 6

Published by
Cheng & Tsui Company, Inc.
25 West Street
Boston, MA 02111-1213 USA
Fax (617) 426-3669
www.cheng-tsui.com
"Bringing Asia to the World"™

Simplified & Traditional Character Edition, ISBN 978-0-88727-539-5

Printed in the United States of America

Chinese Odyssey includes multimedia products, textbooks, workbooks, and audio products. Visit **www.cheng-tsui.com** for more information on the other components of
Chinese Odyssey.

Contents

通向中国

Chinese
Odyssey

Innovative Chinese Courseware

SIMPLIFIED Character

Vol. 1 • WORKBOOK

Xueying Wang, Li-chuang Chi, and Liping Feng

王学英　　　祁立庄　　　冯力平

CHENG & TSUI COMPANY Boston

3
你爸爸妈妈好吗?
How's Your Family?

 听说练习 (Tīng Shuō Liànxí)
Listening/Speaking Exercises

To complete the exercises in this section, you need either the audio CDs or multimedia CD-ROMs. If you have the audio CDs, follow the instructions below. If you have the multimedia CD-ROMs, follow their instructions (no hard copy necessary).

TASK 1. PHRASES AND SENTENCES

The following phrases will be read to you in Chinese, but in a different order than that given below. Demonstrate your understanding of these phrases by numbering their English counterparts in the order in which you hear them.

How is Prof. Li?	Good morning, Auntie Hu.
Our teacher	They are very well.
My grandma is also fine.	Goodbye, Uncle Li.
How about your parents?	How about your grandpa?
Hi!	

TASK 2. SHORT CONVERSATIONS

Listen to the following short conversations and answer the Yes/No questions provided.

Questions

1. Are the ___ ___akers from the same family?   Yes/No

2. Is class about to begin soon?   Yes/No

3. Does the man know the woman's family?   Yes/No

11

TASK 3. SUBSTITUTION

Familiarize yourself with basic sentence patterns by substituting the given phrases into the following sentences. Your audio CDs will include the pronunciation of these sentences. When you finish this exercise, see if you can apply its vocabulary and grammar in your responses to the supplementary questions given on the audio CD.

1. A: 你好。
   B: （史老师）好。

   胡阿姨　　　李阿姨

2. A: （你爸爸妈妈）好吗？
      你爷爷奶奶　林叔叔李阿姨
   B: 他们很好。

3. A: （你爸爸妈妈）呢？
      爷爷奶奶　　史叔叔吴阿姨
   B: （我爸爸妈妈）也很好。

4. A: 再见。
   B: （史老师），再见。

   胡叔叔　　　李叔叔

TASK 4. QUICK RESPONSE

In real conversation, it is important not only to be able to understand the other person, but also to be able to respond in a timely manner. The following exercises will challenge your listening abilities and help you to develop good conversational skills.

Listen to the following sentences and provide a response for each. If you don't know a word, try to get its meaning from the context, rather than looking it up. Remember, both speed and accuracy are important for this exercise!

A. Responding to a Greeting

1. 你好。

2. 再见。

B. Answering a Question

1. 你爸爸妈妈好吗？

2. 你爷爷奶奶呢？

4
好久不见，你怎么样？
How's It Going?

 听说练习 (Tīng Shuō Liànxí)
Listening/Speaking Exercises

 TASK 1. PHRASES AND SENTENCES

The following phrases will be read to you in Chinese, but in a different order than that given below. Demonstrate your understanding of these phrases by numbering their English counterparts in the order in which you hear them.

A. Words/Phrases

Mr. or husband	not serious	too busy
still okay	Mrs. or wife	dad
long time no see	health	mom

B. Sentences

How are you doing?

How is school?

His health is so-so.

They are doing very well with their work.

Everybody is busy and tired.

Our studies are very stressful.

He is doing OK in school.

He is not busy with school, nor with his job.

He is very good at his job, but his health is not so good.

🎧💻 TASK 2. SHORT CONVERSATIONS

Listen to the following short conversations and determine if each statement is true or false.

Questions

1. The man and the woman see each other frequently.   True/False
2. The person mentioned in the dialogue studies very hard.   True/False
3. The man's mother is perfectly healthy, but works too hard.   True/False
4. The woman's father is currently very busy with his work.   True/False
5. The persons mentioned are not stressed out over their work.   True/False

🎧💻 TASK 3. SUBSTITUTION

Familiarize yourself with basic sentence patterns by substituting the given phrases into the following sentences. Your audio CDs will include the pronunciation of these sentences. When you finish this exercise, see if you can apply its vocabulary and grammar in your responses to the supplementary questions given on the audio CD.

1. A: 你(工作)怎么样？

   B: 还好。

   学习   身体

2. A: (你们)学习太忙，也太认真。

   B: 是啊，(我们)都很累。

   大家   他们

3. A: (你爸爸妈妈) 怎么样？

   B: 他们工作都很(忙)。

   李叔叔吴阿姨   紧张
   史老师胡老师   顺利

4. A: 你(先生)身体好吗？

   B: (马马虎虎)。

   太太   还好
   爷爷奶奶   不太好。

5

你做什么工作？

How Do You Make a Living?

 听说练习 (Tīng Shuō Liànxí)
Listening/Speaking Exercises

 TASK 1. PHRASES AND SENTENCES

The following phrases will be read to you in Chinese, but in a different order than that given below. Demonstrate your understanding of these phrases by numbering their English counterparts in the order in which you hear them.

A. Words/Phrases

quite a lot	(medical) Doctor Li	whose boss?
to do business	our teacher	his doctor
to specialize in computers	engineer	her nurse

B. Sentences

What does your friend do?

Neither of my parents is in business.

These are all my computers.

What is this?

You don't have many questions.

Whose books are those?

What does he specialize in?

Is that his boss?

Which one of you is Professor Hu?

🎧💻 TASK 2. SHORT CONVERSATIONS

Listen to the short conversations and select the correct answer.

1. The speakers are talking about
    a) a teacher.　　　　　b) each other.　　　　　c) several teachers.

2. The books mentioned in the conversation belong to
    a) the male speaker.　　b) the female speaker.　c) neither of them.

3. The person mentioned has
    a) one job.　　　　　　b) two jobs.　　　　　　c) three jobs.

4. The person mentioned has
    a) no doctor.　　　　　b) one doctor.　　　　　c) more than one doctor.

🎧💻 TASK 3. SUBSTITUTION

Familiarize yourself with the basic sentence patterns by substituting the given phrases into the following sentences. Your audio CDs will include the pronunciation of these sentences. When you finish this exercise, see if you can apply its vocabulary and grammar in your responses to the supplementary questions given on the audio CD.

1. A: 你们谁是（大夫）？

   B: 我们都不是（大夫）。
   医生　　　护士

2. A: 你（叔叔）做什么工作？

   B: 我（叔叔）搞电脑，也做生意。
   朋友　　　哥哥

3. A: 他的（朋友）很多。

   B: 是吗？我的（朋友）也不少。
   问题　　　书

4. A: 那是谁的（电脑）？

   B: 那是我（老板）的（电脑）。
   书　　　老师
   老板　　　朋友

🎧💻 TASK 4. QUICK RESPONSE

A. Questions & Answers

Listen to the following questions and provide an answer to each one. If you don't know a word, try to get its meaning from the context, rather than looking it up. Remember, both speed and accuracy are important!

1. 那是谁？
2. 你朋友都做生意吗？
3. 你爸爸妈妈做什么工作？
4. 你哥哥也搞电脑吗？

B. Turning Positive into Negative

Listen to the previously recorded responses and change each statement into a negative sentence.

1. 我妈妈做生意。
2. 我爸爸也是医生。
3. 这是我哥哥的老师。
4. 他们的书都很多。

 读写练习(Dú Xiě Liànxí)
Reading/Writing Exercises

 TASK 1. ANALYTICAL READING

Demonstrate your understanding of the following text by choosing the best of three choices to replace each of the numbers throughout the passage.

我是(1)。学习很忙，也很累。我妈妈是医生。(2)很忙，她还学习。但是(3)不累，身体(4)好。我爸爸做生意，他生意很多，也很顺利。他(5)还好。我爷爷奶奶(6)做生意。(7)都是老师，他们工作不紧张，(8)身体不太好。

1. 学生   老师   医生
2. 学习   工作   身体
3. 她   他   他们
4. 都   太   很
5. 学习   工作   身体
6. 都不   都   不都
7. 她   他   他们
8. 也是   都是   但是

 ## TASK 2. SHORT PASSAGE

Read the following text and see how well you can answer the True/False questions that follow.

这是我朋友大文。他学电脑。他的电脑书很多，电脑也不少。他学习很紧张。他爸爸妈妈也是我叔叔的好朋友。他爸爸做电脑生意，他爸爸的电脑公司不大，但是，他们公司生意很好。他妈妈是护士。他爸爸妈妈身体都很好。工作也都很顺利。

Supplementary Vocabulary

| 1. | 公司 | gōngsī | n. | company |
| 2. | 大 | dà | adj. | big, large, great |

Questions

1. The writer is a computer science student.   True/False

2. The writer's family knows Dawen's family very well.   True/False

3. The writer's family owns a business.   True/False

4. Nobody in Dawen's family is doing very well.   True/False

TASK 3. DIALOGUE CONSTRUCTION

Using the following situations, create two-line conversations that include the given Chinese words.

1. Ask for someone's occupation.

    a) 什么
    b) 工程师

2. Ask about whether a pile of books on the desk belongs to someone.

    a) 都是   书
    b) 是啊   多

3. Ask about someone's teacher.

    a) 老师   谁
    b) Last name + 教授

4. Ask to whom the computers belong.

    a) 谁的   电脑
    b) 老板   不少

 TASK 4. E-MAIL

You have been trying to get your Chinese program to work for an hour with no success. As you sit there staring at the computer, you recall an old friend, with whom you haven't spoken in years, who is currently studying computer technology. E-mail your friend, asking about family members and friends (note that, since you haven't seen each other in so long, you have to be polite). In particular, ask if your friend knows anyone in the computer business who might be able to help you with your predicament.

7

欢迎你们常来!

Welcoming Guests

 听说练习 (Tīng Shuō Liànxí)
Listening /Speaking Exercises

 TASK 1. PHRASES AND SENTENCES

The following phrases will be read to you in Chinese, but in a different order than that given below. Demonstrate your understanding of these phrases by numbering their English counterparts in the order in which you hear them.

A. Phrases

good tea

please come in

many guests

to eat fruit

to bring presents

very good candy

please take a seat

so many snacks

to have some tea

B. Sentences

He drinks very good Chinese tea.

Visit us often.

Thank you for giving us such good coffee.

Would you like to have Chinese tea or Japanese tea?

I don't eat fruit or snacks.

Everyone please sit down.

You are very kind to bring us so many presents.

Do you drink white wine or red wine?

I have both tea and coffee.

🎧💻 TASK 2. SHORT CONVERSATIONS

Listen to the short conversations and determine if each statement is true or false.

1. The man's brother only likes tea.   True/False

2. The woman is a guest and the man is a host.   True/False

3. The man does not have what the woman wants.   True/False

4. The woman is eager to eat what the man is offering her.   True/False

🎧💻 TASK 3. SUBSTITUTION

Familiarize yourself with basic sentence patterns by substituting the given phrases into the following sentences. Your audio CDs will include the pronunciation of these sentences. When you finish this exercise, see if you can apply its vocabulary and grammar in your responses to the supplementary questions given on the audio CD.

1. A: 你们都有什么（茶）？
   B: 我们（中国茶、英国茶）都有。
      糖   红糖、白糖
      咖啡   法国咖啡、日本咖啡

2. A: 您带这么好的（礼物），谢谢您。
   B: （不用谢）一点儿小意思。
      茶   谢 什么
      点心   别客气

3. A: 您（喝）什么？（红酒）还是（白酒）？
   B: （红酒），（白酒）我都不（喝）。
      搞   工程   电脑
      说   中文   法文

4. A: 你现在（吃点心）还是（吃水果）？
   B: 我都（吃）。谢谢。
      看中文笔记   看中文书
      喝水   喝茶

8

问姓名
Asking Someone's Name

 听力练习 (Tīnglì Liànxí)
Listening Exercises

 TASK 1. PHRASES AND SENTENCES

The following phrases will be read to you in Chinese, but in a different order than that given below. Demonstrate your understanding of these phrases by numbering their English counterparts in the order in which you hear them.

A. Phrases

to have a lot of experience

Chinese students studying outside of China

never mind

to teach Chinese

what I mean is

to be from which part of China

to make a fool of oneself

to not know him

Chinese name

to speak Chinese often

not bad/quite good

to not understand culture

I apologize

to know his name

therefore

to ask questions

B. Sentences

What does your friend call you?

Among all of you, whose last name is Hu?

Excuse me, what is your honorable surname?

Which country is he from?

Do you know him?

Are you a foreign student?

My teacher calls me Lili.

Where is your teacher from?

What is your name?

 TASK 2. SHORT CONVERSATIONS

Listen to the short conversations and answer the Yes/No questions.

1. Do the two speakers know each other?   Yes/No

2. Does the woman know Prof. Li's nationality?   Yes/No

3. Does the man know who the woman's Chinese teacher is?   Yes/No

4. Does the man think that the woman asks too many questions? Yes/No

 TASK 3. DIALOGUE

Listen to the short dialogue and determine if each statement is true or false.

1. The two speakers know each other very well.   True/False

2. The woman is now studying computer science at college. True/False

3. The man is a student.   True/False

4. The man is not Li Dawen's friend.   True/False

TASK 4. MONOLOGUE

Listen to the passage and answer the questions below.

Questions

1. What is the main point of this passage?
   a) The speaker does not like Xiao Gao.
   b) The speaker is introducing his friend Xiao Gao.
   c) The speaker has not seen Xiao Gao for a long time.
   d) None of the above.

2. Which of the following statements is NOT correct?

   a) Xiao Gao sometimes helps the speaker.

   b) Xiao Gao's English is not very good.

   c) Xiao Gao is too shy to ask questions.

   d) None of the above.

3. Which statement best describes Xiao Gao?

   a) He is very smart.

   b) He is a hard-working student.

   c) He knows computers well.

   d) All of the above.

4. Which of the following statements is correct?

   a) The speaker believes that anyone who asks too many questions is not smart.

   b) The speaker is better at computer science than Xiao Gao.

   c) The speaker frequently helps Xiao Gao with his English.

   d) None of the above.

 口语练习 (Kǒuyǔ Liànxí)

Speaking Exercises

 TASK 1. SUBSTITUTION

Familiarize yourself with basic sentence patterns by substituting the given phrases into the following sentences. Your audio CDs will include the pronunciation of these sentences. When you finish this exercise, see if you can apply its vocabulary and grammar in your responses to the supplementary questions given on the audio CD.

1. A: 请问，（你叫什么名字）？

  B: （我）姓谢，叫谢文。

    他姓什么？叫什么？   他

    你朋友的名字是什么   我朋友

2. A: 你（汉语）很不错。

  B: 哪里，哪里，我认识很多（中国）朋友，常常说（汉语）。

    英语   美国   英语

    日语   日本   日语

3. A: 你常(问老师问题)吗？

   B: 不，我不常(问问题)

   教朋友电脑   教电脑

   借同学笔记   借笔记

4. A: 对不起，我(不懂这是什么意思)。

   B: 没关系，(我教你)。

   不懂中国文化   你去看看书

   没有经验   你去问一问

5. A: (张老师)是哪国人？

   B: 是(中国)人。

   A: 她是(中国)哪里人？

   B: (北京)人。

   他太太 日本 东京

   你朋友 美国 纽约

Supplementary Vocabulary

1. 东京 Dōngjīng *n.* Tokyo

2. 纽约 Niǔyuē   *n.* New York

 TASK 2. QUICK RESPONSE

A. Providing a Response

Listen to the following questions and provide an answer to each one. If you don't know a word, try to get its meaning from the context, rather than looking it up. Remember, both speed and accuracy are important!

1. 请问，您贵姓？

2. 你们老师姓什么，叫什么？

3. 你是哪里人？

4. 对不起，我问题太多，是吗？

B. Asking a Question

Listen to the following statements and follow the hints in the right-hand column to ask a related question for each one.

                                                    Hints

1. 他是中国人。   （哪国）

2. 我的中国朋友常常叫我小张。   （什么）

3. 我们汉语老师是张老师。   （谁）

4. 我们老师是上海人。   （哪里人）

🎧📓 TASK 3. GUIDED ROLE-PLAYING

Listen to the following dialogues between two native speakers. Select Role A or Role B and have a dialogue with the computer. After familiarizing yourself with the conversation, construct and record your own dialogue by replacing as many words as possible with related terms. Be creative, but be careful not to disrupt the structure of the conversation!

A. Making Friends

A: 你好。你也是学生吗？

B: 是啊。我学工程。你呢？

A: 我学汉语。我的名字叫谢友。谢谢的"谢"。
      朋友的"友"。你叫什么？

B: 我姓张，叫迎。我的朋友都叫我小张。

A: 你汉语很不错。

B: 哪里，哪里。

B. Where Is He From?

A: 请问，那是史老师吗？

B: 不是。他姓林。

A: 林老师是哪国人？

B: 他是中国人。

A: 他是中国哪儿的人？四川人还是上海人？

B: 四川人，上海人他都不是。他是北京人。

TASK 4. PICTURE DESCRIPTION

Describe the pictures below using the grammar and the vocabulary you learned in this lesson. Use your imagination!

1.

2.

3.

9

找人
Looking for Someone

听力练习(Tīnglì Liànxí)
Listening Exercises

 TASK 1. PHRASES AND SENTENCES

The following phrases will be read to you in Chinese, but in a different order than that given below. Demonstrate your understanding of these phrases by numbering their English counterparts in the order in which you hear them.

A. Phrases

student dorm

to look for trouble

to live at/in which place?

to go together

to be downstairs

such a beautiful car

how many floors?

her roommate

to be embarrassed / I am embarrassed

to be at whose place?

this floor

what number on the second floor?

that classmate/schoolmate

telephone number

must come and have fun

at my place (over there)

B. Sentences

He lives in building 627, number 805, on the eighth floor.

Your friend lives on which floor?

What is the room number?

Where does your brother live?

She is still living with her mom?

Excuse me, is Mr. Li in?

Your car is not here; it's at his place (over there).

Sorry to have bothered you.

Who has my Chinese book?

Doesn't he live in a student dorm?

 TASK 2. SHORT CONVERSATIONS

Listen to the short conversations and answer the Yes/No questions.

1. Did the woman give the man her phone number?   Yes/No

2. Did Wu Wende move to Lin Di's place?   Yes/No

3. Did the woman use the man's phone?   Yes/No

4. Does Dawen live in building 561, room 802?   Yes/No

 TASK 3. DIALOGUE

Listen to the short dialogues and determine if each statement is true or false.

1. The conversation takes place outside building 832.   True/False

2. The man looking for Li Lili went to the wrong building.

        True/False

3. The female speaker in the conversation does not know Li Lili.

        True/False

4. Li Lili and the female speaker live in the same building.

        True/False

 TASK 4. MONOLOGUE

Listen to the passage and answer the questions below.

Questions

1. What does the speaker's friend Dawen do for a living?

    a) He is a student.   b) He works in a student dorm.

    c) He is a teacher.   d) None of the above.

2. How does the speaker know Dawen?

   a) They are friends.

   b) They barely know each other.

   c) They are roommates.

   d) None of the above.

3. Which of the following is correct?

   a) The speaker and Dawen live in the same building.

   b) Dawen and Lin Di live in the same building.

   c) The speaker and Lin Di live in the same building.

   d) None of the above.

4. How well does the speaker know Lin Di?

   a) They know each other very well.

   b) They barely know each other.

   c) The speaker has never heard of Lin Di.

   d) None of the above.

 口语练习(Kǒuyǔ Liànxí)
Speaking Exercises

 TASK 1. SUBSTITUTION

Familiarize yourself with basic sentence patterns by substituting the given phrases into the following sentences. Your audio CDs will include the pronunciation of these sentences. When you finish this exercise, see if you can apply its vocabulary and grammar in your responses to the supplementary questions given on the audio CD.

1. A: 请问，（李叔叔）在吗？

   B: 他不在。他在（高阿姨）那儿。

   张老师　　　　　　学生
   高先生　　　　　　朋友

2. A: 你住哪儿？

   B: 我住学生宿舍（九二五）楼，（二）层，（三）号。

五十四　　六　　九

四〇二　　三　　八

3. A: （史老师）在哪儿？

   B: 我不知道，你去（林老师）那儿找找吧。

   高先生　　　吴先生

   吴阿姨　　　李叔叔

4. A: 他现在在哪儿（休息）？

   B: 他一定在他（朋友）那儿（休息）。

   工作　　　　叔叔

   学习　　　　哥哥

5. A: 我用一下儿你的（电话），好吗？

   B: 我的（电话）在（那儿），你用吧。

   笔记　　　　这儿

   车　　　　　我的室友那儿

🎧💻 TASK 2. QUICK RESPONSE

A. Providing a Response

Listen to the following questions and provide an answer to each one. If you don't know a word, try to get its meaning from the context, rather than looking it up. Remember, both speed and accuracy are important!

1. 请问，你找谁？

2. 请问，李丽莉住这儿吗？ (negative response)

3. 你的电话号是多少？

4. 你的车在哪儿？我用一下儿，好吗？

B. Asking a Question

Listen to the following statements and follow the hints in the right-hand column to ask a related question for each one.

10

介绍朋友
Introducing Friends

 听力练习 (Tīnglì Liànxí)
Listening Exercises

 TASK 1. PHRASES AND SENTENCES

The following phrases will be read to you in Chinese, but in a different order than that given below. Demonstrate your understanding of these phrases by numbering their English counterparts in the order in which you hear them.

A. Phrases

to go shopping

to be very busy lately

to have no girlfriend

to go and visit my mom

her boyfriend

to come and see me

our school

to go with us

to go to a Chinese restaurant

to have or not have time

to have no class in the afternoon

to certainly have class in the morning

to go to the store today

to have supper/dinner

to give you an introduction

to relax a little

B. Sentences

Are you going to be busy tomorrow morning?

Are you going to China to visit your friend?

Is it okay if we go shopping tomorrow?

Her car is beautiful, and her name sounds pretty.

Is he going to the cafe with us?

Are you and your friend going to a restaurant to eat?

You have your Chinese class this afternoon, isn't that right?

Let's go and relax a bit this evening, okay?

Please introduce us to each other.

TASK 2. SHORT CONVERSATIONS

Listen to the short conversations and answer the Yes/No questions.

1. Does the woman know Dayong?   Yes/No
2. Is the woman going to dinner with the man?   Yes/No
3. Is the woman going to have coffee with the man tonight?   Yes/No
4. Does the woman want to go shopping?   Yes/No

TASK 3. DIALOGUE

Listen to the short dialogues and determine if each statement is true or false.

1. Both of the speakers know Li Lili and Chen Dayong.   True/False
2. The two speakers attended the same school.   True/False
3. The woman knows more people than the man.   True/False
4. The woman wants to make more friends.   True/False

TASK 4. MONOLOGUE

Listen to the passage and answer the questions below.

Questions

1. What is this dialogue about?
    a) The narrator wants to introduce Dawen and his sister to everyone.
    b) Dawen wants to introduce his sister to all his friends.
    c) Dawen wants to introduce his sister to the narrator.
    d) None of the above.

2. Which one of the following is correct?
    a) Dawen knows the narrator and the narrator's roommate.
    b) Dawen knows the narrator and all of the narrator's friends.

c) Dawen knows the narrator but not his friends.

d) None of the above.

3. When did the narrator plan to have dinner with his friends?

a) One day during the school break.

b) One day while school is in session.

c) The day when Dawen's sister is visiting Dawen.

d) None of the above.

4. Why does the narrator want to invite everyone over for dinner?

a) He wants Dawen to meet with his friends.

b) He wants to get to know Dawen's sister.

c) He wants to get to know Dawen better.

d) None of the above.

 口语练习(Kǒuyǔ Liànxí)
Speaking Exercises

 TASK 1. SUBSTITUTION

Familiarize yourself with basic sentence patterns by substituting the given phrases into the following sentences. Your audio CDs will include the pronunciation of these sentences. When you finish this exercise, see if you can apply its vocabulary and grammar in your responses to the supplementary questions given on the audio CD.

1. A: 你认识不认识我的(室友)？

    B: 不认识，你给我介绍一下儿，好吗？

    女朋友

    男朋友

2. A: 我和朋友现在(去买东西)，你(去不去)？

    B: 好啊，没问题。

    在宿舍喝咖啡   来不来

    去饭馆吃饭   跟不跟我们去

3. A: 你(明天下午)有没有时间？

    B: 我(明天下午)没有时间，我有(中文)课。

    今天晚上   电脑

    明天上午   工程

4. A: 你现在忙不忙，我们一起去(咖啡馆)。

   B: 对不起，我现在很忙。(明天)去吧。

   商店   以后

   饭馆   晚上

5. A: 他(学习)很好，是不是(你朋友)？

   日文   你们学校的学生

   中文   中国人

 TASK 2. QUICK RESPONSE

A. Providing a Response

Listen to the following questions and provide an answer to each one. If you don't know a word, try to get its meaning from the context, rather than looking it up. Remember, both speed and accuracy are important!

1. 好久不见，你最近怎么样？

2. 我和你的朋友还不认识。

3. 你现在跟朋友去哪儿？

4. 我们下午去咖啡馆，你来不来？ (Negative response)

B. Asking a Question

Listen to the following statements and follow the hints in the right-hand column to ask a related question for each one. Try to avoid using the 吗-type question.

	Hints
1. 她人好，学习也好。	(好不好)
2. 他和李丽莉明天下午都有汉语课。	(有没有)
3. 今天晚上陈大勇跟他的女朋友去中国饭馆。	(跟不跟)
4. 我明天一定来看你。	(来不来)

TASK 3. GUIDED ROLE-PLAYING

Listen to the following dialogues between two native speakers. Select Role A or Role B and have a dialogue with the computer. After familiarizing yourself with the conversation, construct and record your own dialogue by replacing as many words as possible with related terms. Be creative, but be careful not to disrupt the structure of the conversation!

A. Introducing People

At a coffee shop.

A: 你们认识不认识？

B: 我们不认识。

A: 我来给你们介绍一下儿。这是我的好朋友张子倩。

B: 你好，我叫小英。我也常常来这儿喝咖啡。

B. Inviting Someone Somewhere

A: 好久不见，你最近怎么样？

B: 马马虎虎。

A: 今天晚上你忙不忙？我们一起去买东西，
好不好？

B: 我今天晚上有很多作业。明天晚上，怎么样？

A: 明天晚上我跟我们同学一起去中国饭馆吃晚饭。
下午行不行？

B: 行，没问题。明天见。

TASK 4. PICTURE DESCRIPTION

Describe the pictures below using the grammar and the vocabulary you learned in this lesson. Use your imagination!
[You bump into a group of students from your school in front of a Chinese bookstore. Some of them you kno w and some of them you don't.]

读写练习(Dú Xiě Liànxí)
Reading/Writing Exercises

💻 TASK 1. ANALYTICAL READING

How are your critical reading skills? Read the following passage and choose the correct words from the choices below to fill in the missing parts. Be careful! In certain contexts, some words may be grammatically correct yet illogical.

这是我的男朋友。你们不(1)他吧。我(2)你们介绍一下儿。他姓张，叫小业。他不是我们学校的学生。他搞电脑。我现在很忙，常在学校学习。所以，他常常(3)我这儿看我。我们今天晚上一起(4)中国饭馆吃晚饭，你们去不去？

1. 懂　　　　知道　　　　认识
2. 给　　　　跟　　　　　和
3. 去　　　　来　　　　　在
4. 去　　　　来　　　　　跟

我(5)我朋友想去咖啡馆，喝咖啡。但是，上午他有课，下午我有课。昨天晚上他(6)找我，我不在。今天晚上我(7)找他，他的室友说我朋友现在在图书馆做作业。我现在去(8)找他。

5. 在　　　　给　　　　　跟
6. 去　　　　来　　　　　在
7. 去　　　　来　　　　　在
8. 那儿　　　这儿　　　　哪儿

Supplementary Vocabulary

1. 想　　　　xiǎng　　　　v.　　to think about; to want to (do sth.)

2. 图书馆　　túshūguǎn　　n.　　library

TASK 2. SHORT PASSAGE

Read the text and answer the questions that follow.

大文的妹妹丽文现在还跟她爸爸妈妈一起住。她很少见大文，所以很想他。丽文名字漂亮，人也聪明。她以后想学中文，还想去中国学习。她知道我们学校的中文老师很好，所以， 她想来我们这儿看看我们学校，也看看大文。刚才我去看大文。他妹妹丽文也在那儿。大文明天早上有课，我明天下午有课。我明天早上给丽文介绍介绍我们学校。丽文很客气。给我很多礼物，有水果，有点心，我很不好意思。但是她说这是她的一点儿小意思。

Supplementary Vocabulary

1. 妹妹	mèimei	*n.*	younger sister
2. 想	xiǎng	*v.*	to think of, miss (someone)
3. 刚才	gāngcái	*n.*	a moment ago

Questions

1. 大文的妹妹丽文是不是也住在学校？　　　　是/不是

2. 大文明天给不给丽文介绍介绍他的学校？给/不给

3. 丽文常来看大文吗？　　　　　　　　　　常/不常

4. 丽文也在她哥哥的学校学习吗？　　　　　在/不在

 TASK 3. SENTENCE CONSTRUCTION

Create your own questions using the following phrases in the "Question" row, and then answer the questions using the words in the "Response" row.

1. Introduce two friends to each other.

    Question:　　认识

    Response:　　介绍

2. Invite a friend to go somewhere with you.

   Question: 去咖啡馆

   Response: 对不起   中文课

3. Invite a friend to go with you to a store tomorrow.

   Question: 明天   商店

   Response: 没问题   一定

4. Ask whether another friend is going to dinner with you and your friend.

   Question: 跟   中国饭馆

   Response: 看他朋友   以后

 ## TASK 4. E-MAIL

You have agreed to host a foreign exchange student, but you don't know anything about him. E-mail the student and introduce yourself. Tell him a little bit about yourself, including details about your family background, what languages you speak, where you live, your profession, etc. Ask the student to tell you a little bit about himself, too. Use your imagination, but be thorough — remember, first impressions count!

通向中國

Chinese Odyssey

Innovative Chinese Courseware

Xueying Wang, Li-chuang Chi, and Liping Feng

王學英　　　祁立莊　　　馮力平

CHENG & TSUI COMPANY Boston

1

Introduction to Chinese Phonetics

 Part 1

To complete the exercises in this section, you need either the audio CDs or multimedia CD-ROMs. If you have the audio CDs, follow the instructions below. If you have the multimedia CD-ROMs, follow their instructions (no hard copy necessary).

TASK 1. MONOSYLLABLES/DISYLLABLES

The following mono- and disyllables will be read to you, but in a different order than that given below. Demonstrate your understanding of these phrases by numbering their written counterparts in the order in which you hear them.

A. Monosyllables

1. nǔ	2. nǚ	3. lù	4. lǚ
5. dè	6. tè	7. wǒ	8. é
9. tái	10. děi	11. mò	12. mǒu
13. bó	14. bào	15. yí	16. yū

B. Disyllables

1. fēiděi	2. dǎodé	3. tuóbèi	4. bēibāo
5. pǎobù	6. wòdǎo	7. láolèi	8. tōudù
9. nǔlì	10. tàinào	11. dìtú	12. mǔnǚ
13. pùbù	14. yīfu	15. fāfú	16. nǎonù

1

TASK 2. PRONUNCIATION DRILLS

Listen carefully to the examples and try to imitate each sound.

A. Monosyllables

1. tè	2. dòu	3. mō	4. náo	5. pài
6. fěi	7. bǐ	8. nuó	9. nǚ	10. lù

B. Disyllables

1. fúyì	2. wǒlái	3. láolèi	4. dútè	5. nálái
6. pápō	7. dàodé	8. lǔlì	9. tūtou	10. fāfú

 TASK 3. SIGHT-READING

Can you recognize the following items? If you can, read aloud and record them. Your sight-reading skills will be measured by your speed and accuracy.

A. Monosyllables

1. fǒu	2. mó	3. pò	4. nǔ	5. lú
6. tè	7. děi	8. nào	9. lái	10. bēi

B. Disyllables

1. pèidài	2. múnǔ	3. dìtú	4. fěibó	5. méi lái
6. nǔlì	7. dútè	8. dàodé	9. tuōluò	10. máimò

 TASK 4. DICTATION

Listen to the dictation items provided on the CD and write them in pinyin with correct tones.

1._____	2._____	3._____	4._____
5._____	6._____	7._____	8._____
9._____	10._____	11._____	12._____
13._____	14._____	15._____	16._____
17._____	18._____	19._____	20._____

Part II

🎧💻 TASK 1. MONOSYLLABLES/DISYLLABLES

The following mono- and disyllables will be read to you, but in a different order than that given below. Demonstrate your understanding of these phrases by numbering their written counterparts in the order in which you hear them.

A. Monosyllables

1. shǎn	2. shén	3. zhàn	4. chàng
5. rén	6. shéng	7. chē	8. chī
9. cáng	10. sāng	11. rì	12. rè
13. rǎn	14. rǎng	15. cōng	16. zǒng

B. Disyllables

1. réngrán	2. cóngróng	3. shēngchǎn	4. shàngshēng
5. zhànzhēng	6. chángchéng	7. sǒngrán	8. shēnshì
9. cèshēn	10. sòngzǐ	11. céngcì	12. cóngshì
13. zìcǐ	14. cāngsāng	15. chènshān	16. shānshàng

🎧💻 TASK 2. PRONUNCIATION DRILLS

Listen carefully to the examples and try to imitate each sound.

A. Monosyllables

1. zhì	2. chè	3. shī	4. rè	5. zǐ
6. sān	7. céng	8. shén	9. chàng	10. zhōng

B. Disyllables

1. réngrán	2. zhōngshēng	3. céngcì	4. cóngshì	5. shānshàng
6. chūrù	7. zèngsòng	8. chènshān	9. chūcāo	10. cèsuǒ

TASK 3. SIGHT-READING

Can you recognize the following items? If you can, read aloud and record them. Your sight-reading skills will be measured by your speed and accuracy.

A. Monosyllables

1. rán   2. sōng   3. càn   4. cáng   5. shēn

6. zěn   7. zhěng   8. chī   9. chóng   10. zhǒng

B. Disyllables

1. cāngsāng   2. zìcǐ   3. chènshān   4. róngzǒng   5. zhànzhēng

6. shēnshān   7. chángchéng 8. shèngzhǐ   9. réngrán   10. shēnchì

 TASK 4. DICTATION

Listen to the dictation items provided on the CD and write them in pinyin with correct tones.

1._____   2._____   3._____   4._____

5._____   6._____   7._____   8._____

9._____   10._____   11._____   12._____

13._____   14._____   15._____   16._____

17._____   18._____   19._____   20._____

 Part III

 TASK 1. MONOSYLLABLES/DISYLLABLES

The following mono- and disyllables will be read to you, but in a different order than that given below. Demonstrate your understanding of these phrases by numbering their written counterparts in the order in which you hear them.

A. Monosyllables

1. huà	2. guān	3. wēng	4. kūn
5. guì	6. huài	7. wáng	8. huáng
9. guǎ	10. wèn	11. guāng	12. gǔn
13. guǎi	14. kuī	15. wān	16. hún

B. Disyllables

1. huánghuò	2. kuàihuó	3. gōngguān	4. kuàihūn
5. huángguā	6. kuīkòng	7. guǎngkuò	8. guānguāng
9. huánwán	10. kuàguó	11. wǎnhūn	12. wǒguó
13. guǐguài	14. wēnnuǎn	15. wēngwēng	16. wèihūn

🎧💻 TASK 2. PRONUNCIATION DRILLS

Listen carefully to the examples and try to imitate each sound.

A. Monosyllables

1. kuài	2. guǎng	3. wèn	4. huà	5. wēng
6. guǐ	7. guāi	8. wáng	9. kuān	10. kūn

B. Disyllables

1. gōngguān	2. huángguā	3. kuīkòng	4. kuàguó	5. wēngwēng
6. wǎnhūn	7. guǎngkuò	8. guǐguài	9. wēnnuǎn	10. wèihūn

🎧💻 TASK 3. SIGHT-READING

Can you recognize the following items? If you can, read aloud and record them. Your sight-reading skills will be measured by your speed and accuracy.

A. Monosyllables

1. huā	2. wèn	3. huí	4. gǔn	5. guǎn
6. wēng	7. wéi	8. huáng	9. kuài	10. kuì

B. Disyllables

1. kuīkòng	2. wǎnhūn	3. wēngwēng	4. wèiguó	5. wēnnuǎn
6. huángguā	7. huǒguō	8. kuānkuò	9. guǐguài	10. kǔguā

 TASK 4. DICTATION

Listen to the dictation items provided on the CD and write them in pinyin with correct tones.

1. _____   2. _____   3. _____   4. _____

5. _____   6. _____   7. _____   8. _____

9. _____   10. _____   11. _____   12. _____

13. _____   14. _____   15. _____   16. _____

17. _____   18. _____   19. _____   20. _____

 Part IV

 TASK 1. MONOSYLLABLES/DISYLLABLES

The following mono- and disyllables will be read to you, but in a different order than that given below. Demonstrate your understanding of these phrases by numbering their written counterparts in the order in which you hear them.

A. Monosyllables

1. qiū	2. jià	3. qián	4. xǔ
5. jiě	6. xiǎo	7. quán	8. qiáo
9. xiǎng	10. xún	11. xióng	12. qìn
13. quē	14. qìng	15. yǒu	16. qǐ

B. Disyllables

1. jiǎjiè	2. xiǎoxīn	3. quēxiàn	4. xiánxiá
5. jiějué	6. xuánxū	7. xuéxí	8. xīngqī
9. jiǔyuè	9. jiūjìng	10. qiǎngxiān	11. jìnxiū
11. juānqū	12. qīqiè	13. qièqǔ	14. qǔjué

🎧💻 TASK 2. PRONUNCIATION DRILLS

Listen carefully to the examples and try to imitate each sound.

A. Monosyllables

1. yě	2. quē	3. xuán	4. jiū	5. qiàn
6. xiá	7. qiāng	8. xióng	9. jǐn	10. xǐng

B. Disyllables

1. jiějué	2. jiǔyuè	3. qǔjué	4. jìnxiū	5. xíngjūn
6. xīyān	7. jīngjiǎn	8. qiúqíng	9. jìnxìng	10. qiǎngxiān

🎧💻 TASK 3. SIGHT-READING

Can you recognize the following items? If you can, read aloud and record them. Your sight-reading skills will be measured by your speed and accuracy.

A. Monosyllables

1. quē	2. jùn	3. quán	4. jìn	5. jìng
6. qiú	7. xiǎo	8. xiān	9. xióng	10. yāng

B. Disyllables

1. quēxiàn	2. jūnxùn	3. quànjiǔ	4. juānxiàn	5. jíjù
6. xìqǔ	7. qiǎngxiān	8. xióngxīn	9. qǐng jìn	10. xiūxi

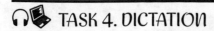 TASK 4. DICTATION

Listen to the dictation items provided on the CD and write them in pinyin
with correct tones.

1. _____   2. _____   3. _____   4. _____

5. _____   6. _____   7. _____   8. _____

9. _____   10. _____   11. _____   12. _____

13. _____   14. _____   15. _____   16. _____

17. _____   18. _____   19. _____   20. _____

2
你早
Basic Greetings

 TASK 1. PINYIN PRACTICE

Practice your tones and pronunciation by listening to a native speaker on your audio CD or multimedia CD-ROM. If you have the multimedia CD-ROM, record yourself reading each item and then check your recording against the voice of the native speaker.

1. Nǐ zǎo.   2. Nǐ hǎo.   3. Nín zǎo.

4. Nín hǎo.   5. Lǎoshī hǎo.   6. Lǎoshī zǎo.

 TASK 2. SIGHT-READING

Can you recognize the following items? If you can, read aloud and record them. Your sight-reading skills will be measured by your speed and accuracy. If you need help, double click the pinyin on your multimedia CD-ROM and the computer will read it for you.

1. lín   2. nín   3. zī

4. shǐ   5. Lǎoshī hǎo.   6. hǎo lǎoshī

7. Lǎoshī zǎo.   8. Nín zǎo, Shí Lǎoshī.

 TASK 3. STROKE ORDER PRACTICE

Try to discern the stroke order of the characters provided. Practice by writing each of the characters in the correct stroke order, numbering the strokes as you write them.

你　早　老
師　您　好

 TASK 4. RADICAL RECOGNITION

How well do you know the radicals? Look at the characters below and circle
the radical in each of them.

你　　早　　您　　好

3

你爸爸媽媽好嗎？
How's Your Family?

 聽說練習 (Tīng Shuō Liànxí)
Listening/Speaking Exercises

To complete the exercises in this section, you need either the audio CDs or multimedia CD-ROMs. If you have the audio CDs, follow the instructions below. If you have the multimedia CD-ROMs, follow their instructions (no hard copy necessary).

 TASK 1. PHRASES AND SENTENCES

The following phrases will be read to you in Chinese, but in a different order than that given below. Demonstrate your understanding of these phrases by numbering their English counterparts in the order in which you hear them.

How is Prof. Li?   Good morning, Auntie Hu.

Our teacher   They are very well.

My grandma is also fine.   Goodbye, Uncle Li.

How about your parents?   How about your grandpa?

Hi!

 TASK 2. SHORT CONVERSATIONS

Listen to the following short conversations and answer the Yes/No questions provided.

Questions

1. Are the two speakers from the same family?   Yes/No

2. Is class about to begin soon?   Yes/No

3. Does the man know the woman's family?   Yes/No

11

🎧💻 TASK 3. SUBSTITUTION

Familiarize yourself with basic sentence patterns by substituting the given phrases into the following sentences. Your audio CDs will include the pronunciation of these sentences. When you finish this exercise, see if you can apply its vocabulary and grammar in your responses to the supplementary questions given on the audio CD.

1. A: 你好。
   B: （史老師）好。
      胡阿姨　　　李阿姨

2. A: （你爸爸媽媽）好嗎？
   B: 他們很好。
      你爺爺奶奶　林叔叔李阿姨

3. A: （你爸爸媽媽）呢？
   B: （我爸爸媽媽）也很好。
      爺爺奶奶　　史叔叔吳阿姨

4. A: 再見。
   B: （史老師），再見。
      胡叔叔　　　李叔叔

🎧💻 TASK 4. QUICK RESPONSE

In real conversation, it is important not only to be able to understand the other person, but also to be able to respond in a timely manner. The following exercises will challenge your listening abilities and help you to develop good conversational skills.

Listen to the following sentences and provide a response for each. If you don't know a word, try to get its meaning from the context, rather than looking it up. Remember, both speed and accuracy are important for this exercise!

A. Responding to a Greeting

1. 你好。   2. 再見。

B. Answering a Question

1. 你爸爸媽媽好嗎？   2. 你爺爺奶奶呢？

讀寫練習(Dú Xiě Liànxí)
Reading/Writing Exercises

 TASK 1. FILL IN THE BLANKS

Fill in the blanks in this dialogue by taking a word from below and placing it appropriately in the sentence.

呢 嗎 也很 很

A: 你爸爸媽媽好_____？

B: 他們_____好。

A: 你爺爺奶奶_____？

B: 他們_____好。

 TASK 2. SHORT PASSAGE

Read the following text and answer the True/False questions that follow.

A: 您早，胡叔叔。

B: 你早，吳文德。

A: 李阿姨好嗎？

B: 她很好。你爸爸媽媽呢？

A: 他們也很好。

　　· · · · · ·

A: 胡叔叔再見。

B: 再見，吳文德。

Questions

1. In this dialogue, the speakers have asked each other about five different people. True/False

2. In this conversation, "他們" refers to 胡叔叔 and 李阿姨.　　　True/False

TASK 3. CHARACTER WRITING PRACTICE

A. Radical Recognition

How well do you know the radicals? Look at the characters below and circle the radical in each of them.

B. Stroke Order

Try to discern the stroke order of the characters provided. Practice by writing each of the characters in the correct stroke order, numbering the strokes as you write them.

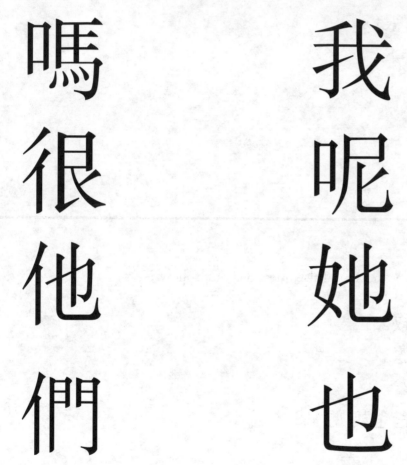

嗎　　我
很　　呢
他　　她
們　　也

 TASK 4. DIALOGUE CONSTRUCTION

Use the following patterns learned in this lesson to construct a dialogue of at least four lines.

1. Last Name + 阿姨/叔叔/爺爺/奶奶.

2. A pronoun with a term indicating relationship.

3. 嗎 and 呢.

4
好久不見，你怎麼樣？
How's It Going?

 聽說練習 (Tīng Shuō Liànxí)
Listening/Speaking Exercises

 TASK 1. PHRASES AND SENTENCES

The following phrases will be read to you in Chinese, but in a different order than that given below. Demonstrate your understanding of these phrases by numbering their English counterparts in the order in which you hear them.

A. Words/Phrases

Mr. or husband	not serious	too busy
still okay	Mrs. or wife	dad
long time no see	health	mom

B. Sentences

How are you doing?

How is school?

His health is so-so.

They are doing very well with their work.

Everybody is busy and tired.

Our studies are very stressful.

He is doing OK in school.

He is not busy with school, nor with his job.

He is very good at his job, but his health is not so good.

🎧💻 TASK 2. SHORT CONVERSATIONS

Listen to the following short conversations and determine if each statement is true or false.

Questions

1. The man and the woman see each other frequently.   True/False
2. The person mentioned in the dialogue studies very hard.   True/False
3. The man's mother is perfectly healthy, but works too hard. True/False
4. The woman's father is currently very busy with his work. True/False
5. The persons mentioned are not stressed out over their work. True/False

🎧💻 TASK 3. SUBSTITUTION

Familiarize yourself with basic sentence patterns by substituting the given phrases into the following sentences. Your audio CDs will include the pronunciation of these sentences. When you finish this exercise, see if you can apply its vocabulary and grammar in your responses to the supplementary questions given on the audio CD.

1. A: 你(工作)怎麼樣?

   B: 還好。

   學習   身體

2. A: (你們)學習太忙,也太認真。

   B: 是啊,(我們)都很累。

   大家   他們

3. A: (你爸爸媽媽)怎麼樣?

   B: 他們工作都很(忙)。

   李叔叔吳阿姨   緊張
   史老師胡老師   順利

4. A: 你(先生)身體好嗎?

   B: (馬馬虎虎)。

   太太   還好

   爺爺奶奶   不太好

TASK 4. QUICK RESPONSE

Listen to the following sentences and provide a response for each. If you don't
know a word, try to get its meaning from the context, rather than looking it
up. Remember, both speed and accuracy are important for this exercise!

Recorded Statement	Your Response
我學習很累。	我學習不累。

1. 她學習太緊張。

2. 我工作學習都很順利。

3. 他工作認真，學習也很好。

4. 高先生身體很好，李太太身體也很好。

 讀寫練習 (Dú Xiě Liànxí)
Reading/Writing Exercises

 TASK 1. ANALYTICAL READING

How are your critical reading skills? Read the following passage and choose the
correct words from the choices below to fill in the missing parts. Be careful! In
certain contexts, some words may be grammatically correct yet illogical.

A: 吳文德，好久不見。你(1)？

B: 我還好，你呢？你學習(2)？

A: 很忙。我們大家(3)都很緊張。

B: 你爸爸工作順利(4)？

A: 我爸爸(5)順利，但是，太忙，太累。

B: 你媽媽(6)？她身體好嗎？

A: 她(7)好。你爸爸媽媽怎麼樣？

B: 他們工作(8)都很忙，但是，身體都很好。

1. 呢　　　　嗎　　　　怎麼樣
2. 忙嗎　　　忙呢　　　太忙
3. 認真　　　學習　　　身體
4. 呢　　　　嗎　　　　怎麼樣
5. 學習　　　工作　　　身體
6. 呢　　　　嗎　　　　很好嗎
7. 都　　　　也　　　　還
8. 都　　　　也　　　　還

TASK 2. SHORT PASSAGE

Read the following letter and answer the questions that follow.

吳文德，你好。

你怎麼樣？學習很緊張嗎？我現在身體還好。但是學習馬馬虎虎。我哥哥工作很累，也很緊張，他身體也不太好。我爸爸媽媽總是很忙。但是他們工作都很順利，身體也很好。你爸爸媽媽呢？他們好嗎？再見！

祝你學習順利！

林笛

Supplementary Vocabulary

1. 現在　　xiànzài　　*adv.*　　now
2. 哥哥　　gēge　　　*n.*　　　elder brother
3. 總是　　zǒngshì　　*adv.*　　always
4. 祝　　　zhù　　　　*v.*　　　to wish

Questions

1. What is the relationship between Wu Wende and Lin Di?
   a) colleagues　　　　　b) friends
   c) siblings　　　　　　d) teacher-student

2. When was this letter written?
   a) summer break   b) in the morning
   c) winter break   d) during school
3. Who is Lin Di?
   a) a teacher   b) a student
   c) a health care worker d) teacher and student
4. Who is the most unfortunate person mentioned in the letter?
   a) Wu Wende   b) Wu Wende's parents
   c) Lin Di   d) Lin Di's brother

TASK 3. SENTENCE CONSTRUCTION

Create dialogues for each of the following situations. Make up questions based on the guidelines provided. Then answer the questions using the given words. As a bonus, challenge yourself by trying to use at least two words or phrases that carry similiar meanings to those given below.

1. Ask about someone's work. Use the given word to
   provide a response.   累

2. Ask about someone's classes. Use the given words to
   provide a response.   不太緊張

3. Ask about someone's health using 怎麼樣. Use the
   given words to provide a response.   還好

TASK 4. E-MAIL

Now it is time for you to learn how to use a Chinese word processor to input pinyin and produce Chinese characters. Send an e-mail in Chinese to your friend who also studies Chinese. That friend goes to a different school, and you haven't seen each other for a long time; find out how your friend is. How are studies going? Is school OK? How is the family?

5

你做什麼工作?
How Do You Make a Living?

 聽說練習 (Tīng Shuō Liànxí)
Listening/Speaking Exercises

 TASK 1. PHRASES AND SENTENCES

The following phrases will be read to you in Chinese, but in a different order than that given below. Demonstrate your understanding of these phrases by numbering their English counterparts in the order in which you hear them.

A. Words/Phrases

quite a lot   (medical) Doctor Li   whose boss?

to do business   our teacher   his doctor

to specialize in computers   engineer   her nurse

B. Sentences

What does your friend do?

Neither of my parents is in business.

These are all my computers.

What is this?

You don't have many questions.

Whose books are those?

What does he specialize in?

Is that his boss?

Which one of you is Professor Hu?

21

🎧💻 TASK 2. SHORT CONVERSATIONS

Listen to the short conversations and select the correct answer.

1. The speakers are talking about
   a) a teacher.   b) each other.   c) several teachers.

2. The books mentioned in the conversation belong to
   a) the male speaker.   b) the female speaker.   c) neither of them.

3. The person mentioned has
   a) one job.   b) two jobs.   c) three jobs.

4. The person mentioned has
   a) no doctor.   b) one doctor.   c) more than one doctor.

🎧💻 TASK 3. SUBSTITUTION

Familiarize yourself with the basic sentence patterns by substituting the given phrases into the following sentences. Your audio CDs will include the pronunciation of these sentences. When you finish this exercise, see if you can apply its vocabulary and grammar in your responses to the supplementary questions given on the audio CD.

1. A: 你們誰是(大夫)？

   B: 我們都不是(大夫)。
   　　醫生　　　護士

2. A: 你(叔叔)做什麼工作？

   B: 我(叔叔)搞電腦，也做生意。
   　　朋友　　　哥哥

3. A: 他的(朋友)很多。

   B: 是嗎？我的(朋友)也不少。
   　　問題　　　書

4. A: 那是誰的(電腦)？

   B: 那是我(老闆)的(電腦)。
   　　書　　　　老師
   　　老闆　　　朋友

🎧💻 TASK 4. QUICK RESPONSE

A. Questions & Answers

Listen to the following questions and provide an answer to each one. If you don't know a word, try to get its meaning from the context, rather than looking it up. Remember, both speed and accuracy are important!

1. 那是誰？
2. 你朋友都做生意嗎？
3. 你爸爸媽媽做甚麼工作？
4. 你哥哥也搞電腦嗎？

B. Turning Positive into Negative

Listen to the previously recorded responses and change each statement into a negative sentence.

1. 我媽媽做生意。
2. 我爸爸也是醫生。
3. 這是我哥哥的老師。
4. 他們的書都很多。

 讀寫練習(Dú Xiě Liànxí)

Reading/Writing Exercises

 TASK 1. ANALYTICAL READING

Demonstrate your understanding of the following text by choosing the best of three choices to replace each of the numbers throughout the passage.

我是(1)。學習很忙，也很累。我媽媽是醫生。(2)很忙，她還學習。但是 (3)不累，身體 (4) 好。我爸爸做生意，他生意很多，也很順利。他 (5)還好。 我爺爺奶奶(6)做生意。(7)都是老師，他們工作不緊張，(8)身體不太 好。

1. 學生　　　老師　　　醫生
2. 學習　　　工作　　　身體
3. 她　　　　他　　　　他們
4. 都　　　　太　　　　很
5. 學習　　　工作　　　身體
6. 都不　　　都　　　　不都
7. 她　　　　他　　　　他們
8. 也是　　　都是　　　但是

 TASK 2. SHORT PASSAGE

Read the following text and see how well you can answer the True/False questions that follow.

這是我朋友大文。他學電腦。他的電腦書很多，
電腦也不少。他學習很緊張。他爸爸媽媽也是我
叔叔的好朋友。他爸爸做電腦生意，他爸爸的電腦
公司不大，但是，他們公司生意很好。他媽媽是護
士。他爸爸媽媽身體都很好。工作也都很順利。

Supplementary Vocabulary

1. 公司　　　gōngsī　　　n.　　　company
2. 大　　　　dà　　　　　adj.　　　big, large, great

Questions

1. The writer is a computer science student.　　　True/False

2. The writer's family knows Dawen's family very well.　　　True/False

3. The writer's family owns a business.　　　True/False

4. Nobody in Dawen's family is doing very well.　　　True/False

TASK 3. DIALOGUE CONSTRUCTION

Using the following situations, create two-line conversations that include the given Chinese words.

1. Ask for someone's occupation.

   a) 什麼
   b) 工程師

2. Ask about whether a pile of books on the desk belongs to someone.

   a) 都是　　書
   b) 是啊　　多

3. Ask about someone's teacher.

   a) 老師　　誰
   b) Last name + 教授

4. Ask to whom the computers belong.

   a) 誰的　　電腦
   b) 老闆　　不少

 ## TASK 4. E-MAIL

You have been trying to get your Chinese program to work for an hour with no success. As you sit there staring at the computer, you recall an old friend, with whom you haven't spoken in years, who is currently studying computer technology. E-mail your friend, asking about family members and friends (note that, since you haven't seen each other in so long, you have to be polite). In particular, ask if your friend knows anyone in the computer business who might be able to help you with your predicament.

6

做作業
Doing Homework

 聽說練習 (Tīng Shuō Liànxí)
Listening/Speaking Exercises

 TASK 1. PHRASES AND SENTENCES

The following phrases will be read to you in Chinese, but in a different order than that given below. Demonstrate your understanding of these phrases by numbering their English counterparts in the order in which you hear them.

A. Words/Phrases

to speak Chinese   to take a break

confused   very smart

to do homework   thank you

to borrow (sth.) for a second   to read a book

to use for a little while

B. Sentences

The homework is very difficult, right?

I am not using it now, so you can use it.

Is it all right with you if I borrow your notes for the Chinese class?

You are very smart.

I am returning the Chinese notes.

Where are you going now?

I'm very confused today.

Today's homework is not too difficult.

Do you still want to take a break?

TASK 2. SHORT CONVERSATIONS

Listen to the short conversations and determine if each statement is true or false.

1. The man is still using his notes.   True/False

2. The man is still reading his book.   True/False

3. The man did not help the woman with her homework.   True/False

4. The woman has succeeded in borrowing the item she needs.   True/False

---

TASK 3. SUBSTITUTION

Familiarize yourself with basic sentence patterns by substituting the given phrases into the following sentences. Your audio CDs will include the pronunciation of these sentences. When you finish this exercise, see if you can apply its vocabulary and grammar in your responses to the supplementary questions given on the audio CD.

1. A: 我們（說說中文），怎麼樣？
    B: 好吧。
    休息休息　　　　看看書

2. A: 你現在去哪兒？
    B: 我去（還書）。
    借筆記　　　　做作業

3. A: 他很（聰明），是嗎？
    B: 是啊，你也很（聰明）。
    糊塗　　　　認真

4. A: 你來（看書中文），對嗎？
    B: 對啊，你來做什麼？
    A: 我來（用）一下兒（電腦）。
    還書　　　　問　　　　問題
    借書　　　　看　　　　吳文德的筆記

🎧💻 TASK 4. QUICK RESPONSE

A. Providing a Response

Listen to the following questions and provide an answer to each one. If you don't know a word, try to get its meaning from the context, rather than looking it up. Remember, both speed and accuracy are important!

1. 你很聰明，也很認真，對嗎？

2. 你現在去哪兒？

3. 你現在用你的筆記嗎？

4. 今天你的作業很多，也很難，是嗎？

B. Asking a Question

Listen to the following statements and follow the hints in the right-hand column to ask a related question for each one.

Hints

1. 我去休息休息。　　　　　　　　　（做什麼）

2. 我現在不用我的中文書。你用吧。　（還用嗎）

3. 好吧。你現在來看看我的作業。　　（好嗎）

4. 他去還書。　　　　　　　　　　　（哪兒）

讀寫練習 (Dú Xiě Liànxí)
Reading/Writing Exercises

💻 TASK 1. ANALYTICAL READING

Read the following passage. For each number in the dialogue, choose the best of the three given options to complete the sentence in question.

A: 你現在去(1)？你(2)做中文作業嗎？

B: 我(3)做，學習太累，去休息休息。

A: 我用一下兒你的中文書，(4)？

B: 好啊。(5)現在不用。

A: 你的中文筆記(6)？你現在還(7)嗎？

B: 我也不用。你用(9)。

A: 謝謝。

1. 甚麼　　　　　　哪兒　　　　　　誰
2. 也　　　　　　　太　　　　　　　還
3. 都　　　　　　　不　　　　　　　也
4. 好嗎　　　　　　嗎　　　　　　　呢
5. 你　　　　　　　我　　　　　　　他
6. 呢　　　　　　　嗎　　　　　　　吧
7. 還　　　　　　　借　　　　　　　用
8. 呢　　　　　　　嗎　　　　　　　吧

 ## TASK 2. SHORT PASSAGE

Read the passage and see how well you can answer the multiple choice questions that follow.

我學習很緊張，也很累，我很想休息休息。但是我現在得做作業。今天的中文作業很多，也很難。老師的問題我都不懂。我的朋友聰明，學習也很認真。她現在不用她的中文課筆記，我想借一下兒她的筆記。我還想看看她的作業。但是她說她不借我她的作業，只借我她的筆記。她還說我不懂，她教我。唉，我快累死了。

Supplementary Vocabulary

1.	想	xiǎng	v.	to want to do something
2.	得	dé	aux.	to have to do something
3.	只	zhǐ	adj.	only

Questions

1. What is the main point of this passage?

    a) The writer does not want to do any Chinese homework.

    b) The writer lacks energy to finish his Chinese homework.

    c) The writer's friend does not want to lend him anything.

    d) None of the above.

2. How many items did the writer borrow from his friend?

    a) one

    b) two

    c) three

    d) four

 TASK 3. DIALOGUE CONSTRUCTION

Use the vocabulary and grammar learned so far to create three dialogues (three to four lines each) based on the following topics.

Topic 1.　　借筆記（借書）

Topic 2.　　我的中文課

Topic 3.　　今天的作業

 TASK 4. E-MAIL

Your friend borrowed an item from you and still hasn't given it back. E-mail your friend and ask if he or she is done using it, explain why you need it back, and determine whether you can have it back today.

7

歡迎你們常來！
Welcoming Guests

 聽說練習 (Tīng Shuō Liànxí)
Listening / Speaking Exercises

 TASK 1. PHRASES AND SENTENCES

The following phrases will be read to you in Chinese, but in a different order than that given below. Demonstrate your understanding of these phrases by numbering their English counterparts in the order in which you hear them.

A. Phrases

good tea   please come in

many guests   to eat fruit

to bring presents   very good candy

please take a seat   so many snacks

to have some tea

B. Sentences

He drinks very good Chinese tea.

Visit us often.

Thank you for giving us such good coffee.

Would you like to have Chinese tea or Japanese tea?

I don't eat fruit or snacks.

Everyone please sit down.

You are very kind to bring us so many presents.

Do you drink white wine or red wine?

I have both tea and coffee.

TASK 2. SHORT CONVERSATIONS

Listen to the short conversations and determine if each statement is true or false.

1. The man's brother only likes tea.   True/False

2. The woman is a guest and the man is a host.   True/False

3. The man does not have what the woman wants.   True/False

4. The woman is eager to eat what the man is offering her.   True/False

TASK 3. SUBSTITUTION

Familiarize yourself with basic sentence patterns by substituting the given phrases into the following sentences. Your audio CDs will include the pronunciation of these sentences. When you finish this exercise, see if you can apply its vocabulary and grammar in your responses to the supplementary questions given on the audio CD.

1. A: 你們都有什麼(茶)？
   B: 我們(中國茶、英國茶)都有。

   糖   紅糖, 白糖
   咖啡   法國咖啡, 日本咖啡

2. A: 您帶這麼好的(禮物)，謝謝您。
   B: (不用謝)一點兒小意思。

   茶   謝什麼
   點心   別客氣

3. A: 您(喝)什麼？(紅酒)還是(白酒)？
   B: (紅酒)，(白酒)我都不(喝)。

   搞   工程   電腦
   說   中文   法文

4. A: 你現在(吃點心)還是(吃水果)？
   B: 我都(吃)。謝謝。

   看中文筆記   看中文書
   喝水   喝茶

🎧💻 TASK 4. QUICK RESPONSE

A. *Providing a Response*

Listen to the following questions and provide an answer to each one. If you don't know a word, try to get its meaning from the context, rather than looking it up. Remember, both speed and accuracy are important!

1. 你喝中國咖啡還是日本咖啡？ (negative response)

2. 你們有什麼茶？

3. 這是你的禮物。

4. 您帶這麼好的禮物！謝謝，謝謝！

B. *Asking a Question*

Listen to the following statements and follow the hints in the right-hand column to ask a related question for each one.

	Hints
1. 中國茶日本茶我們都有。	（還是）
2. 謝謝。我不吃糖。	（嗎）
3. 我們有點心，也有水果。	（什麼）
4. 我吃水果，我先生吃點心。	（誰）

 讀寫練習 (Dú Xiě Liànxí)

Reading/Writing Exercises

TASK 1. ANALYTICAL READING

How are your critical reading skills? Read the following passage and choose the correct words from the choices below to fill in the missing parts. Be careful! In certain contexts, some words may be grammatically correct yet illogical.

麗莉，

你好。好久不見，你現在 (1)？學習順利嗎？
學習(2)太認真。學習認真太累。我哥哥明天
請客。 他的朋友, 我的朋友都 (3)。你來嗎？
我哥哥現在是工程師，工作很忙，很緊張。他
常常不休息， 也不吃飯。茶, 咖啡他 (4)喝。
但是，他常常吃 (5)點心，還常常吃糖。我爸
爸媽媽都說吃點心，吃糖(6)不好。明天 我哥
哥做 (7)，他做的中國飯，日本飯(8)吃。你
來吧。但是，別帶禮物！ 好吧。
明天見！

大文

Supplementary Vocabulary

1.	明天	míngtiān	*n.*	tomorrow
2.	請客	qǐngkè	*v.*	to treat sb. to sth. (dinner, etc.)
3.	飯	fàn	*n.*	food

Choices

1.	很好	不忙	怎麼樣
2.	別	不	很
3.	去	來	有
4.	不也太	也不太	太不也
5.	很多	多	多的
6.	多太	太多不	太多
7.	中國的飯	中國飯	中國
8.	都很好	很都好	很好都

TASK 2. SHORT PASSAGE

Read the passage and see how well you can answer the multiple choice questions that follow.

明天我休息，不學習。我去我的好朋友家吃法國飯。我帶什麼禮物？帶茶還是帶咖啡？ 我想，茶, 咖啡都不好。他現在不應該喝太多茶，也不應該喝太多咖啡。茶, 咖啡我現在也都不喝。我帶糖吧。我有很好的日本糖。但是，他吃糖不多。帶糖也不好。我帶中文筆記吧。他常借我的筆記。但是，我的筆記不是禮物。 我想我明天不帶禮物，怎麼樣？

Supplementary Vocabulary

1.　家　　　jiā　　　*v.*　　　home

2.　想　　　xiǎng　　*v.*　　　to think

3.　應該　　yīnggāi　*aux.*　　should

Questions

1. What is the writer concerned about?
   a) Whether or not to accept his friend's invitation.
   b) Whether to bring tea or coffee as a present.
   c) What present to take to his friend.
   d) None of the above.

2. What does the writer drink these days?
   a) Coffee but not tea.
   b) Tea but not coffee.
   c) Neither tea nor coffee.
   d) Both tea and coffee.

3. What present will the writer take to his friend?
   a) Coffee and tea.
   b) Candy.
   c) His notebook.
   d) None of the above.

4. Which one of the following statements is correct?
    a) The writer thinks that tea is good for one's health.
    b) The writer does not know his friend very well.
    c) The writer is very busy with schoolwork.
    d) None of the above.

 ## TASK 3. DIALOGUE CONSTRUCTION

Create a short dialogue (at least six lines) based on the following situation.
A host is entertaining several guests at his home. He offers different kinds
of drinks to the guests, and in return, they bring him nice gifts as a gesture
of appreciation. Create a dialogue between the host and the guests covering
three major areas: welcoming guests, hosting guests, and saying goodbye to
guests.

 ## TASK 4. E-MAIL

You have just had a fantastic party, but your best friend was out of town and
missed it. Tell your friend all about the party in an e-mail.

8
問姓名
Asking Someone's Name

 聽力練習 (Tīnglì Liànxí)
Listening Exercises

 TASK 1. PHRASES AND SENTENCES

The following phrases will be read to you in Chinese, but in a different order than that given below. Demonstrate your understanding of these phrases by numbering their English counterparts in the order in which you hear them.

A. Phrases

to have a lot of experience	Chinese students studying outside of China
never mind	to teach Chinese
what I mean is	to be from which part of China
to make a fool of oneself	to not know him
Chinese name	to speak Chinese often
not bad/quite good	to not understand culture
I apologize	to know his name
therefore	to ask questions

B. Sentences

What does your friend call you?

Among all of you, whose last name is Hu?

Excuse me, what is your honorable surname?

Which country is he from?

Do you know him?

Are you a foreign student?

My teacher calls me Lili.

Where is your teacher from?

What is your name?

 TASK 2. SHORT CONVERSATIONS

Listen to the short conversations and answer the Yes/No questions.

1. Do the two speakers know each other?   Yes/No

2. Does the woman know Prof. Li's nationality?   Yes/No

3. Does the man know who the woman's Chinese teacher is?   Yes/No

4. Does the man think that the woman asks too many questions?   Yes/No

---

 TASK 3. DIALOGUE

Listen to the short dialogue and determine if each statement is true or false.

1. The two speakers know each other very well.   True/False

2. The woman is now studying computer science at college. True/False

3. The man is a student.   True/False

4. The man is not Li Dawen's friend.   True/False

 TASK 4. MONOLOGUE

Listen to the passage and answer the questions below.

Questions

1. What is the main point of this passage?
    a) The speaker does not like Xiao Gao.
    b) The speaker is introducing his friend Xiao Gao.
    c) The speaker has not seen Xiao Gao for a long time.
    d) None of the above.

2. Which of the following statements is NOT correct?

   a) Xiao Gao sometimes helps the speaker.

   b) Xiao Gao's English is not very good.

   c) Xiao Gao is too shy to ask questions.

   d) None of the above.

3. Which statement best describes Xiao Gao?

   a) He is very smart.

   b) He is a hard-working student.

   c) He knows computers well.

   d) All of the above.

4. Which of the following statements is correct?

   a) The speaker believes that anyone who asks too many questions is not smart.

   b) The speaker is better at computer science than Xiao Gao.

   c) The speaker frequently helps Xiao Gao with his English.

   d) None of the above.

 口語練習 (Kǒuyǔ Liànxí)

Speaking Exercises

 TASK 1. SUBSTITUTION

Familiarize yourself with basic sentence patterns by substituting the given phrases into the following sentences. Your audio CDs will include the pronunciation of these sentences. When you finish this exercise, see if you can apply its vocabulary and grammar in your responses to the supplementary questions given on the audio CD.

1. A: 請問，(你叫什麼名字)？

   B: (我)姓謝，叫謝文。

   　他姓什麼？叫什麼？　　　　他

   　你朋友的名字是什麼　　　　我朋友

2. A: 你(漢語)很不錯。

   B: 哪裡，哪裡，我認識很多(中國)朋友，常常說(漢語)。

   　英語　　　　　美國　　　　英語

   　日語　　　　　日本　　　　日語

3. A: 你常(問老師問題)嗎？

 B: 不，我不常(問問題)。

 教朋友電腦　　　　　教電腦

 借同學筆記　　　　　借筆記

4. A: 對不起，我(不懂這是什麼意思)。

 B: 沒關係，(我教你)。

 不懂中國文化　　　　你去看看書

 沒有經驗　　　　　　你去問一問

5. A: (張老師)是哪國人？

 B: 是(中國)人。

 :她是(中國)哪裡人？

 B: (北京)人。

 他太太　　　　日本　　　東京

 你朋友　　　　美國　　　紐約

Supplementary Vocabulary

1. 東京　　Dōngjīng　　*n.*　　Tokyo

2. 紐約　　Niǔyuē　　*n.*　　New York

🎧💻 TASK 2. QUICK RESPONSE

A. Providing a Response

Listen to the following questions and provide an answer to each one. If you don't know a word, try to get its meaning from the context, rather than looking it up. Remember, both speed and accuracy are important!

1. 請問，您貴姓？

2. 你們老師姓　麼，叫什麼？

3. 你是哪裡人？

4. 對不起，我問題太多，是嗎？

B. Asking a Question

Listen to the following statements and follow the hints in the right-hand column to ask a related question for each one.

Hints

1. 他是中國人。　　　　　　　　　（哪國）

2. 我的中國朋友常常叫我小張。　　（什麼）

3. 我們漢語老師是張老師。　　　　（誰）

4. 我們老師是上海人。　　　　　　（哪裡人）

🎧💻 TASK 3. GUIDED ROLE-PLAYING

Listen to the following dialogues between two native speakers. Select Role A or Role B and have a dialogue with the computer. After familiarizing yourself with the conversation, construct and record your own dialogue by replacing as many words as possible with related terms. Be creative, but be careful not to disrupt the structure of the conversation!

A. Making Friends

A:　　你好。你也是學生嗎？

B:　　是啊。我學工程。你呢？

A:　　我學漢語。我的名字叫謝友。謝謝的"謝"。朋友的"友"。你叫什麼？

B:　　我姓張，叫迎。我的朋友都叫我小張。

A:　　你漢語很不錯。

B:　　哪裡，哪裡。

B. Where Is He From?

A:　　請問，那是史老師嗎？

B:　　不是。他姓林。

A:　　林老師是哪國人？

B:　　他是中國人。

A:　　他是中國哪兒的人？四川人還是上海人？

B:　　四川人，上海人他都不是。他是北京人。

TASK 4. PICTURE DESCRIPTION

Describe the pictures below using the grammar and the vocabulary you learned in this lesson. Use your imagination!

1.

2.

3.

讀寫練習(Dú Xiě Liànxí)
Reading/Writing Exercises

 TASK 1. SHORT PASSAGE

Read the text and answer the questions that follow.

馬明是我哥哥的朋友，你認識他嗎？他在我們學校
教書，教工程。他哥哥馬文也是我們學校的老師，
教電腦。但是我不認識馬文。學生現在叫馬文大馬
老師，叫馬明小馬老師。但是，很多學生不認識
他們，不知道誰是大馬老師，誰是小馬老師。
學生常常來問他：您是大馬老師還是小馬老師？
馬明常常開玩笑說他哥哥不應該姓馬，應該姓王。
中國人很多人都姓王。那樣，學生都叫他哥哥王老師。

Supplementary Vocabulary

1.	馬明	Mǎ Míng	*n.*	a person's name
2.	馬文	Mǎ Wén	*n.*	a person's name
3.	在	zài	*prep.*	at, in
4.	應該	yīnggāi	*aux.*	should
5.	那樣	nàyàng	*adj.*	like that, that way

Questions

1. 大馬老師和小馬老師都是我的朋友。   True/False
2. 學生認識大馬老師但是不認識小馬老師。

                                                     True/False

3. 小馬老師常常鬧笑話。   True/False
4. 學生現在叫大馬老師王老師。   True/False

🖥 TASK 2. AUTHENTIC MATERIALS

In this section, you will be exposed to some authentic Chinese materials.
Read the business cards and answer the following questions.

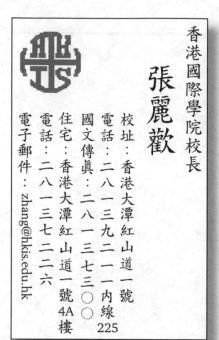

香港國際學院校長

張麗歡

校址：香港大潭紅山道一號
電話：二八一三九二一一內線
國文傳眞：二八一三九二一一內線
住宅：香港大潭紅山道一號
電話：二八一三七二二六
電子郵件：zhang@hkis.edu.hk

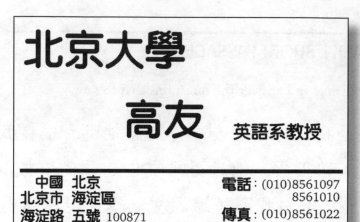

北京大學

高友　英語系教授

中國　北京
北京市　海淀區
海淀路　五號　100871

電話：(010)8561097
　　　　　 8561010
傳眞：(010)8561022

中國電腦公司

謝迎英　工程師

地址：中國・上海
　　　成門外大街
郵編：100037

電話：(021)6832.7534
　　　(021)6876.2351
傳眞：(021)6876.7535

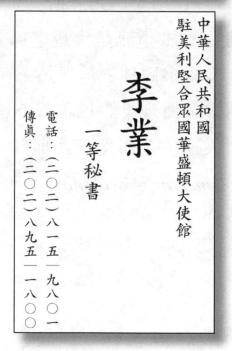

中華人民共和國
駐美利堅合眾國華盛頓大使館

李業

一等秘書

電話：(二○二)八一五一九八○一
傳眞：(二○二)八九五一一八○○

Questions

1. What are the last names of the people on the business cards? Write them down.

2. Of the four business cards, which one is the engineer? What is the engineer's last name?

3. Of the four business cards, one of them is a professor. How do you address the professor?

4. Who is the principal of Hong Kong International School? Please write down the principal's name.

TASK 3. SENTENCE CONSTRUCTION

Create your own questions using the following phrases in the "Question" row, and then answer the questions using the words in the "Response" row.

1. Ask for someone's Chinese name.
   Question: 名字
   Response: 姓   叫

2. Ask for someone's place of origin.
   Question: 朋友   哪裡
   Response: 四川

3. Ask someone how he or she is called by others.
   Question: 叫   你
   Response: 叫   我

4. Inquire if someone frequently asks questions.
   Question: 常常   問題
   Response: 是啊   多

TASK 4. E-MAIL

You've just met a fellow student who is also studying Chinese. When you return to your dorm, you decide to e-mail that student to find out if he or she is interested in studying with you sometime soon. To make sure that the student remembers who you are, you should introduce yourself again. Also ask the student for the names and surnames of his or her teachers. Have you had any of the same teachers? Say what you know about your teachers.

9
找人
Looking for Someone

 聽力練習 (Tīnglì Liànxí)
Listening Exercises

 TASK 1. PHRASES AND SENTENCES

The following phrases will be read to you in Chinese, but in a different order than that given below. Demonstrate your understanding of these phrases by numbering their English counterparts in the order in which you hear them.

A. Phrases

student dorm	to be embarrassed / I am embarrassed
to look for trouble	to be at whose place?
to live at/in which place?	this floor
to go together	what number on the second floor?
to be downstairs	that classmate/schoolmate
such a beautiful car	telephone number
how many floors?	must come and have fun
her roommate	at my place (over there)

B. Sentences

He lives in building 627, number 805, on the eighth floor.

Your friend lives on which floor?

What is the room number?

Where does your brother live?

She is still living with her mom?

Excuse me, is Mr. Li in?

Your car is not here; it's at his place (over there).

Sorry to have bothered you.

Who has my Chinese book?

Doesn't he live in a student dorm?

TASK 2. SHORT CONVERSATIONS

Listen to the short conversations and answer the Yes/No questions.

1. Did the woman give the man her phone number?   Yes/No

2. Did Wu Wende move to Lin Di's place?   Yes/No

3. Did the woman use the man's phone?   Yes/No

4. Does Dawen live in building 561, room 802?   Yes/No

TASK 3. DIALOGUE

Listen to the short dialogues and determine if each statement is true or false.

1. The conversation takes place outside building 832.   True/False

2. The man looking for Li Lili went to the wrong building.

      True/False

3. The female speaker in the conversation does not know Li Lili.

      True/False

4. Li Lili and the female speaker live in the same building.

      True/False

TASK 4. MONOLOGUE

Listen to the passage and answer the questions below.

Questions

1. What does the speaker's friend Dawen do for a living?

   a) He is a student.   b) He works in a student dorm.

   c) He is a teacher.   d) None of the above.

2. How does the speaker know Dawen?

   a) They are friends.

   b) They barely know each other.

   c) They are roommates.

   d) None of the above.

3. Which of the following is correct?

   a) The speaker and Dawen live in the same building.

   b) Dawen and Lin Di live in the same building.

   c) The speaker and Lin Di live in the same building.

   d) None of the above.

4. How well does the speaker know Lin Di?

   a) They know each other very well.

   b) They barely know each other.

   c) The speaker has never heard of Lin Di.

   d) None of the above.

 口語練習 (Kǒuyǔ Liànxí)
Speaking Exercises

 TASK 1. SUBSTITUTION

Familiarize yourself with basic sentence patterns by substituting the given phrases into the following sentences. Your audio CDs will include the pronunciation of these sentences. When you finish this exercise, see if you can apply its vocabulary and grammar in your responses to the supplementary questions given on the audio CD.

1. A: 請問，（李叔叔）在嗎？

   B: 他不在。他在（高阿姨）那兒。

   張老師   學生
   高先生   朋友

2. A: 你住哪兒？

   B: 我住學生宿舍（九二五）樓，（二）層，（三）號。

五十四　　六　　九
四〇二　　三　　八

3. A: （史老師）在哪兒？

   B: 我不知道，你去（林老師）那兒找找吧。

   高先生　　　吳先生
   吳阿姨　　　李叔叔

4. A: 他現在在哪兒（休息）？

   B: 他一定在他（朋友）那兒（休息）。

   工作　　　　叔叔
   學習　　　　哥哥

5. A: 我用一下兒你的（電話），好嗎？

   B: 我的（電話）在（那兒），你用吧。

   筆記　　　　這兒
   車　　　　　我的室友那兒

🎧💻 TASK 2. QUICK RESPONSE

A. Providing a Response

Listen to the following questions and provide an answer to each one. If you don't know a word, try to get its meaning from the context, rather than looking it up. Remember, both speed and accuracy are important!

1. 請問，你找誰？

2. 請問，李麗莉住這兒嗎？ (negative response)

3. 你的電話號是多少？

4. 你的車在哪兒？我用一下兒，好嗎？

B. Asking a Question

Listen to the following statements and follow the hints in the right-hand column to ask a related question for each one.

Hints

1. 我現在住學生宿舍。　　　　　　　（哪兒）
2. 他住四層四十九號。　　　　　　　（幾層多少號）
3. 他的電話是二八六一九五七三。　　（多少）
4. 她不在。她在吳文德那兒。　　　　（嗎）

🎧💻 TASK 3. GUIDED ROLE-PLAYING

Listen to the following dialogues between two native speakers. Select Role A or Role B and have a dialogue with the computer. After familiarizing yourself with the conversation, construct and record your own dialogue by replacing as many words as possible with related terms. Be creative, but be careful not to disrupt the structure of the conversation!

A. *Looking for Someone*

A: 請問，你找誰？

B: 我找李麗莉，我是她的同學。她在嗎？

A: 她現在不在。她在高朋那兒。

B: 高朋的電話號碼是多少？

A: 他的號碼是四三一五七六〇。

B. *Where Does He Live?*

A: 請問，高朋住哪兒？

B: 高朋住學生宿舍七五六樓。

A: 七五六樓幾層？多少號？

B: 四層四十四號。

A: 麻煩你了。我去那兒找他一下兒。再見。

TASK 4. PICTURE DESCRIPTION

Describe the pictures below using the grammar and the vocabulary you learned in this lesson. Use your imagination! [You are asking someone for information about someone's residence.]

1.

2.

3.

讀寫練習 (Dú Xiě Liànxí)
Reading/Writing Exercises

 TASK 1. SHORT PASSAGE

Read the text and answer the questions that follow.

我叫德文，是大文的室友。王德是大文的中國朋友。
他現在常常來我們宿舍玩兒。他常常說：歡迎你們
去我那兒坐坐。有一天，我問他：

你住哪兒？他告訴我：我住學生宿舍八一（yāo）二樓。
我不懂。我問他：八一（yāo）二是什麼意思。我們
這兒沒有八一（yāo）二樓。他說：對不起，你還不知
道。"一"我們中國人常常說" yāo "。你看我的電話
號是六二三五一八一〇五。但是我說：六二三五一
八一（yāo）〇五。所以，八一（yāo）二樓就是學生宿
舍八一（yī）二樓。

Supplementary Vocabulary

1. 有一天   yǒu yītiān   *adj.*   one day
2. 告訴   gàosu   *v.*   to tell

Questions

1. 王德是中國留學生。   True/False
2. 德文不知道王德住哪兒。   True/False
3. 王德告訴德文"yāo"是"一"的意思。
                                        True/False
4. 德义和王德是室友。   True/False

 ## TASK 2. AUTHENTIC MATERIALS

Here is another opportunity for you to read some authentic Chinese materials. Read the business cards and answer the following questions. Can you get all four correct?

1.

香港國際學院校長

張麗歡

校址：香港大潭紅山道一號
電話：二八一三九二一一一內線225
國文傳真：二八一三七三〇〇
住宅：香港大潭紅山道一號4A樓
電話：二八一三七二二六
電子郵件：zhang@hkis.edu.hk

2.

北京大學

高友   英語系教授

中國　北京
北京市　海淀區
海淀路　五號 100871

電話：(010)8561097
　　　　8561010
傳真：(010)8561022

3.

中國電腦公司

謝迎英 工程師

地址：中國・上海   電話：(021) 6832.7534
　　　成門外大街　　　 (021) 6876.2351
郵編：100037   傳真：(021) 6876.7535

4.
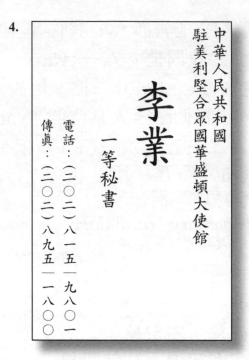

中華人民共和國
駐美利堅合眾國華盛頓大使館

李業
一等秘書

電話：(二〇二) 八一五一九八〇一
傳眞：(二〇二) 八九五一一八〇〇

Questions

1. Which business card lists both the business and home addresses?

2. Whose phone number is 28136226?

3. Who works for a computer company? Can you tell by looking at the card?

4. Which person does not live in China? (Use the process of elimination.)

TASK 3. SENTENCE CONSTRUCTION

Using the following situations, create two-line conversations that incorporate
the given Chinese words.

1. Ask, very politely, if someone is in.

    Question: 在

    Response: 不   她朋友

2. Ask someone for another person's phone number.

    Question: 多少

    Response: 是

3. Look for something, and ask if anyone else has it.

    Question: 誰   那兒

    Response: 不   這兒

4. Inquire if someone is in the dorm.

    Question: 學生宿舍

    Response: Use your real address if applicable. Otherwise, make
                       something up.

 **TASK 4. E-MAIL**

You have a big project coming up, and your partner hasn't contacted you to
work on it. You find his/her name and e-mail address on the class enrollment
list and are trying to contact him/her to meet and go over the assignment. As
you are writing the e-mail, be sure to include information about where you
live, how to contact you, etc. Ask your partner to confirm his/her information
as well. It may take more than one e-mail before you actually get together.

10
介紹朋友
Introducing Friends

 聽力練習 (Tīnglì Liànxí)
Listening Exercises

 TASK 1. PHRASES AND SENTENCES

The following phrases will be read to you in Chinese, but in a different order than that given below. Demonstrate your understanding of these phrases by numbering their English counterparts in the order in which you hear them.

A. Phrases

to go shopping

to be very busy lately

to have no girlfriend

to go and visit my mom

her boyfriend

to come and see me

our school

to go with us

to go to a Chinese restaurant

to have or not have time

to have no class in the afternoon

to certainly have class in the morning

to go to the store today

to have supper/dinner

to give you an introduction

to relax a little

B. Sentences

Are you going to be busy tomorrow morning?

Are you going to China to visit your friend?

Is it okay if we go shopping tomorrow?

Her car is beautiful, and her name sounds pretty.

Is he going to the cafe with us?

Are you and your friend going to a restaurant to eat?

You have your Chinese class this afternoon, isn't that right?

Let's go and relax a bit this evening, okay?

Please introduce us to each other.

 TASK 2. SHORT CONVERSATIONS

Listen to the short conversations and answer the Yes/No questions.

1. Does the woman know Dayong?   Yes/No

2. Is the woman going to dinner with the man?   Yes/No

3. Is the woman going to have coffee with the man tonight?   Yes/No

4. Does the woman want to go shopping?   Yes/No

 TASK 3. DIALOGUE

Listen to the short dialogues and determine if each statement is true or false.

1. Both of the speakers know Li Lili and Chen Dayong.   True/False

2. The two speakers attended the same school.   True/False

3. The woman knows more people than the man.   True/False

4. The woman wants to make more friends.   True/False

 TASK 4. MONOLOGUE

Listen to the passage and answer the questions below.

Questions

1. What is this dialogue about?
    a) The narrator wants to introduce Dawen and his sister to everyone.
    b) Dawen wants to introduce his sister to all his friends.
    c) Dawen wants to introduce his sister to the narrator.
    d) None of the above.

2. Which one of the following is correct?
    a) Dawen knows the narrator and the narrator's roommate.
    b) Dawen knows the narrator and all of the narrator's friends.

c) Dawen knows the narrator but not his friends.

d) None of the above.

3. When did the narrator plan to have dinner with his friends?

a) One day during the school break.

b) One day while school is in session.

c) The day when Dawen's sister is visiting Dawen.

d) None of the above.

4. Why does the narrator want to invite everyone over for dinner?

a) He wants Dawen to meet with his friends.

b) He wants to get to know Dawen's sister.

c) He wants to get to know Dawen better.

d) None of the above.

口語練習 (Kǒuyǔ Liànxí)
Speaking Exercises

 TASK 1. SUBSTITUTION

Familiarize yourself with basic sentence patterns by substituting the given phrases into the following sentences. Your audio CDs will include the pronunciation of these sentences. When you finish this exercise, see if you can apply its vocabulary and grammar in your responses to the supplementary questions given on the audio CD.

1.　A: 你認識不認識我的 (室友)？

　　B: 不認識，你給我介紹一下兒，好嗎？

　　　女朋友

　　　男朋友

2.　A: 我和朋友現在 (去買東西)，你 (去不去)？

　　B: 好啊，沒問題。

　　　在宿舍喝咖啡　　　　　來不來

　　　去飯館吃飯　　　　　　跟不跟我們去

3.　A: 你 (明天下午) 有沒有時間？

　　B: 我 (明天下午) 沒有時間，我有 (中文) 課。

　　　今天晚上　　　　　　電腦

　　　明天上午　　　　　　工程

4. A: 你現在忙不忙，我們一起去(咖啡館)。

   B: 對不起，我現在很忙。(明天)去吧。

   商店　　　　　以後

   飯館　　　　　晚上

5. A: 他(學習)很好，是不是(你朋友)？

   日文　　　　　你們學校的學生

   中文　　　　　中國人

 TASK 2. QUICK RESPONSE

A. Providing a Response

Listen to the following questions and provide an answer to each one. If you don't know a word, try to get its meaning from the context, rather than looking it up. Remember, both speed and accuracy are important!

1. 好久不見，你最近怎麼樣？

2. 我和你的朋友還不認識。

3. 你現在跟朋友去哪兒？

4. 我們下午去咖啡館，你來不來？ (Negative response)

B. Asking a Question

Listen to the following statements and follow the hints in the right-hand column to ask a related question for each one. Try to avoid using the 嗎-type question.

		Hints
1. 她人好，學習也好。		(好不好)
2. 他和李麗莉明天下午都有漢語課。		(有沒有)
3. 今天晚上陳大勇跟他的女朋友去中國飯館。		(跟不跟)
4. 我明天一定來看你。		(來不來)

🎧💻 TASK 3. GUIDED ROLE-PLAYING

Listen to the following dialogues between two native speakers. Select Role A or Role B and have a dialogue with the computer. After familiarizing yourself with the conversation, construct and record your own dialogue by replacing as many words as possible with related terms. Be creative, but be careful not to disrupt the structure of the conversation!

A. *Introducing People*

At a coffee shop.

A: 你們認識不認識？

B: 我們不認識。

A: 我來給你們介紹一下兒。這是我的好朋友張子倩。

B: 你好，我叫小英。我也常常來這兒喝咖啡。

B. *Inviting Someone Somewhere*

A: 好久不見，你最近怎麼樣？

B: 馬馬虎虎。

A: 今天晚上你忙不忙？我們一起去買東西，
好不好？

B: 我今天晚上有很多作業。明天晚上，怎麼樣？

A: 明天晚上我跟我們同學一起去中國飯館吃晚飯。
下午行不行？

B: 行，沒問題。明天見。

TASK 4. PICTURE DESCRIPTION

Describe the pictures below using the grammar and the vocabulary you learned in this lesson. Use your imagination!

[You bump into a group of students from your school in front of a Chinese bookstore. Some of them you know and some of them you don't.]

讀寫練習(Dú Xiě Liànxí)
Reading/Writing Exercises

📖 TASK 1. ANALYTICAL READING

How are your critical reading skills? Read the following passage and choose the correct words from the choices below to fill in the missing parts. Be careful! In certain contexts, some words may be grammatically correct yet illogical.

這是我的男朋友。你們不(1)他吧。我(2)你們介紹一下兒。他姓張，叫小業。他不是我們學校的學生。他搞電腦。 我現在很忙，常在學校學習。所以，他常常(3)我這兒看我。 我們今天晚上一起(4)中國飯館吃晚飯， 你們去不去？

1. 懂   知道   認識
2. 給   跟   和
3. 去   來   在
4. 去   來   跟

我(5)我朋友想去咖啡館，喝咖啡。但是， 上午他有課，下午我有課。昨天晚上他(6)找我，我不在。今天晚上我(7)找他，他的室友說我朋友現在在圖書館做作業。我現在去(8)找他。

5. 在   給   跟
6. 去   來   在
7. 去   來   在
8. 那兒   這兒   哪兒

Supplementary Vocabulary

1. 想   xiǎng   *v.*   to think about; to want to (do sth.)

2. 圖書館   túshūguǎn   *n.*   library

TASK 2. SHORT PASSAGE

Read the text and answer the questions that follow.

大文的妹妹麗文現在還跟她爸爸媽媽一起住。她很
少見大文，所以很想他。麗文名字漂亮，人也聰明。
她以後想學中文，還想去中國學習。她知道我們學
校的中文老師很好，所以，她想來我們這兒，看看
我們學校，也看看大文。　剛才我去看大文。他妹妹
麗文也在那兒。大文明天早上有課，我明天下午有
課。我明天早上給麗文介紹介紹我們學校。麗文很
客氣。給我很多禮物，有水果，有點心，我很不好
意思。但是她說這是她的一點兒小意思。

Supplementary Vocabulary

1. 妹妹   mèimei   *n.*   younger sister

2. 想   xiǎng   *v.*   to think of, miss (someone)

3. 剛才   gāngcái   *n.*   a moment ago

Questions

1. 大文的妹妹麗文是不是也住在學校？   是/不是

2. 大文明天給不給麗文介紹他的學校？   給/不給

3. 麗文常來看大文嗎？   常/不常

4. 麗文也在她哥哥的學校學習嗎？   在/不在

 TASK 3. SENTENCE CONSTRUCTION

Create your own questions using the following phrases in the "Question"
row, and then answer the questions using the words in the "Response" row.

1. Introduce two friends to each other.

   Question: 認識
   Response: 介紹

2. Invite a friend to go somewhere with you.

    Question: 去咖啡館

    Response: 對不起   中文課

3. Invite a friend to go with you to a store tomorrow.

    Question: 明天   商店

    Response: 沒問題   一定

4. Ask whether another friend is going to dinner with you and your friend.

    Question: 跟   中國飯館

    Response: 看他朋友   以後

 TASK 4. E-MAIL

You have agreed to host a foreign exchange student, but you don't know anything about him. E-mail the student and introduce yourself. Tell him a little bit about yourself, including details about your family background, what languages you speak, where you live, your profession, etc. Ask the student to tell you a little bit about himself, too. Use your imagination, but be thorough — remember, first impressions count!